NOTICE: You
Reprin   MW00623940

INTRODUCTION

Before we embark on this journey of time-tested food preservation methods, it's vital to understand why this ancient wisdom still holds value in our modern world. We aren't just talking about keeping your apple pie fresh for a few more days here. We're talking about an insurance policy against times of need, a way to make the most of nature's bounty, and let's not forget, a satisfying hobby that can save you a penny or two!

Food preservation, in its essence, is about delaying the spoilage of food. We're essentially tricking Mother Nature into extending the edible life of our victuals. Now, don't worry - you won't need a degree in biochemistry to understand this process. In simple terms, food preservation techniques slow down the activity of disease-causing bacteria, or in other words, the tiny party-crashers that turn your delicious food into a science experiment gone wrong.

Each method of food preservation - whether it's canning, freezing, curing, or the others we're about to explore - has its unique way of telling these bacteria to take a hike. And these methods do one more crucial thing - they aim to retain as much of the food's original nutrient content as possible. After all, we're in this for the long haul, and we can't compromise on nutrition.

Choosing the right method of preservation isn't a one-size-fits-all solution, my friend. Some foods take well to certain methods and not others. We'll delve deeper into each technique and their suitable food types in the coming chapters.

Now, you might be wondering why we're looking to our ancestors for advice on something as important as food preservation. After all, haven't modern techniques improved and become safer? The truth is, while our forebears might not have had all the fancy gadgets we have today, they had something even more important - time-tested wisdom and experience. Their methods worked, kept families fed through winters, droughts, and times of scarcity, and have been passed down through generations for us to learn and benefit from. As a bonus, these methods are often more natural and sustainable - a win-win if you ask me!

Whether you're a prepper bracing for the next big hurricane, a survivalist training for off-grid living, a homesteader nurturing a self-sufficient lifestyle, or a family looking to stretch your grocery budget and reduce waste, this book is for you.

And remember, as we journey through the world of food preservation together, always consider my favorite motto: "One is none, two is one." In other words, always have a backup. And that applies not only to food supplies but also to knowledge.

In the next chapters, we'll roll up our sleeves and get down to the nitty-gritty of each preservation method. By the end of this book, you'll have the know-how to fill your pantry with preserved foods, just like our ancestors did. So, buckle up, my friend, because we're about to embark on a deliciously rewarding journey!

Chapter One: Understanding Food Preservation

We've had our chit-chat and set the scene for our journey. Now it's time to really sink our teeth into the juicy stuff. And by that, I mean delving into the meat and potatoes of food preservation. Alright, enough with the food metaphors, let's get to it.

At its core, food preservation is simply about making food last longer. It's about delaying the spoilage, so you don't have to throw out that surplus of tomatoes because you couldn't make enough spaghetti sauce to save your life. It's about extending the bounties of summer into the harsh cold of winter. But, most importantly, it's about keeping food safe and nutritious to eat.

You see, there are these pesky little microorganisms, such as bacteria and fungi, that love to feast on our food. The moment a fruit is plucked, a vegetable is harvested, or an animal is butchered, the race begins against these unwanted guests. The goal of food preservation is to win that race by slowing down these tiny party crashers and maintaining as much of the food's original nutritional value as possible.

"But how," you might wonder, "do we achieve such a feat?" Well, that's where our handy dandy preservation methods come in. Each method has its way of making our food less hospitable for bacteria and other spoilage organisms, while keeping the food's nutrients intact.

For instance, freezing slows down the microorganisms because they're like tropical vacationers who hate the cold. Canning kills off these party poopers with heat and then seals the food in a vacuum so no new uninvited guests can get in. Salting and curing draw out the moisture from food to create an environment that's as welcoming to bacteria as a desert is to a fish. You get the idea. We're basically using different methods to make our food a no-fun zone for these spoilage organisms.

The trick, though, lies in choosing the right method for the right food. Not all foods take kindly to all methods. You wouldn't want to salt your strawberries or freeze your honey, right? Don't worry; I'll guide you through the specifics for each method as we progress.

Lastly, you might wonder why it matters if we retain the nutritional content of the food. After all, isn't the main goal just to have food that lasts? Well, my friend, in a survival scenario, you want your food to do more than just fill your belly. You need it to nourish you, keep you healthy, and give you the energy to tackle whatever life throws your way. So, preservation isn't just about longevity; it's about maintaining quality, too.

Alright, I can see you're eager to get started, and who could blame you? In our next section, we'll start uncovering the secrets of our first preservation method: canning. Prepare to get steamy!

Chapter Two: Canning

I hope you're as excited as I am to delve into our first preservation method: canning. Now, canning might seem like a modern invention, what with all the mason jars and fancy pressure canners. But, you might be surprised to learn it's actually been around since the early 19th century.

History and Evolution of Canning

Canning's roots can be traced back to France during the Napoleonic wars. Soldiers needed a reliable way to preserve food for long campaigns, and the French government offered a hefty cash prize for anyone who could come up with a solution.

Enter Nicolas Appert, a candy maker and brewer, who invented a method of preserving food in glass jars sealed with wax and reinforced with wire. Interestingly, Appert didn't fully understand why his method worked - he thought it was the exclusion of air, rather than the heat treatment, that preserved the food. But hey, as long as it worked, right?

Fast forward a few decades, and canning made its way across the pond to the United States, where it was embraced by settlers moving west. They quickly discovered the value of having preserved food on hand in remote areas where fresh food was scarce.

Over the years, canning technology and techniques have evolved and improved. We've swapped out glass jars for tin cans and back to glass again, developed pressure canners for low-acid foods, and learned more about the science behind canning. But the essence of the method remains the same, preserving the tastes of summer to enjoy all year round.

Necessary Equipment and Supplies

Now, before we roll up our sleeves and get to canning, we'll need to gather our gear. Don't worry, though; you won't need to sell a kidney to afford it. Here's what you'll need:

- **Canning Jars:** These are special jars made to withstand the heat of canning. And no, before you ask, that old pickle jar won't do the trick.
- **Lids and Bands**: Lids create the all-important seal that keeps food fresh, while bands hold the lids in place during processing. Remember, lids are one-time use only, but bands can be reused.
- **Canner:** You'll need either a boiling water canner for high-acid foods like jams and pickles or a pressure canner for low-acid foods like vegetables and meats.
- **Jar Lifter:** Unless you have fingers made of steel, you'll want this to lift hot jars out of the canner.
- **Funnel, Ladle, and Bubble Remover:** These will help you fill jars neatly and remove air bubbles.

Step-by-step Process of Canning

Alright, equipment gathered. Apron on. It's canning time! Here's a basic step-by-step process to get you started:

1. Clean and heat your jars.
2. Prepare your food according to your recipe.
3. Fill the jars with food, leaving appropriate headspace.
4. Wipe the rims clean, place the lids on, and screw the bands on finger tight.
5. Process in a canner, either boiling water or pressure, depending on the food.
6. Once processed, let jars cool, check seals, label, and store.

Pat yourself on the back - you're a canner!

Remember, this is just a basic guide. Always follow specific instructions for the food you're canning to ensure safety and quality.

Recipes and Tips for Successful Canning

Now, I bet you're itching to start canning. To send you on your way, here are a couple of my favorite canning recipes: Classic Tomato Sauce and Blue Ribbon Black Berry Jam.

Classic Tomato Sauce

- Ingredients: ripe tomatoes, fresh basil, onions, garlic, olive oil, salt, and lemon juice
- You'll begin by sautéing the onions and garlic in olive oil, adding the tomatoes, and letting it simmer.
- Add some fresh basil, salt, and a squeeze of lemon juice for acidity.
- Fill your jars and process them in a boiling water canner.
- Voila! Summer in a jar.

Blue Ribbon Blackberry Jam

- Ingredients: fresh blackberries, sugar, pectin, and lemon juice
- Crush your berries, combine them with sugar, and bring the mixture to a boil.
- Add your pectin, simmer for a while, and don't forget to skim off any foam.

- Pack the jam into jars and process in a boiling water canner.
- Spread this on toast, and your breakfast will never be the same again.

Canning is both an art and a science, my friend. The science keeps your food safe, while the art makes it delicious. As you continue your canning journey, keep these tips in mind:

- **Always use tested recipes:** Especially as a beginner, don't play around with ratios and ingredients. Botulism is no joke, folks.
- **Acidity matters:** High-acid foods can be processed in a boiling water canner, while low-acid foods need the higher heat of a pressure canner.
- **Don't reuse lids:** Once a lid has been used and sealed once, it's done its job. Bands, however, can be reused.
- **No jar is too small:** If you have a little leftover food that won't fill a jar, pop it in the fridge and enjoy it fresh.
- **Have fun:** Canning is a practical skill, yes, but it's also a creative and satisfying hobby. Enjoy the process as well as the product.

WATER BATH CANNING

Now let's take a look at a method that's ideal for high-acid foods like fruits, jams, and pickles: water bath canning. It's an accessible and reliable way to preserve your harvest, one that our ancestors relied upon and that we can employ in our own kitchens.

The Basics of Water Bath Canning

Water bath canning uses a large pot of boiling water to heat jars filled with high-acid food. Here's a basic step-by-step guide:

- **Prepare Your Ingredients:** Clean, peel, chop, or otherwise prepare your food according to your chosen recipe.
- **Prepare Your Jars and Lids:** Sterilize your jars, lids, and bands by washing in warm, soapy water and then boiling them in a large pot for 10 minutes.
- **Fill Your Jars:** Pack your food into the jars, leaving enough headspace (usually about 1/4 to 1/2 inch) at the top.
- **Seal Your Jars:** Wipe the rim of the jar to ensure a clean seal. Place a sterilized lid on the jar and screw on the band until it's finger-tight.
- **Process Your Jars:** Place your jars in a canner or large pot filled with boiling water. The water should cover the jars by at least 1 inch. Boil for the amount of time specified in your recipe.
- **Cool and Check Your Jars:** Once processed, remove the jars using a jar lifter and let them cool for 12-24 hours. Check that the lids have sealed properly (they should not flex up and down when pressed). Store in a cool, dark place.

Best Foods for Water Bath Canning

Water bath canning is best for high-acid foods. This includes:

- Fruits like apples, peaches, and pears.
- Tomatoes with added acidity (like lemon juice or vinegar).
- Pickled foods such as cucumbers, onions, and beets.
- Jams, jellies, and marmalades.
- Acidic sauces and salsas.
- Water Bath Canning Tips

Here are a few tips to keep in mind as you navigate your water bath canning journey:

- **Adjust for Altitude:** Boiling point decreases as altitude increases, so you may need to adjust your processing time if you live at a high altitude.
- **Ensure a Good Seal:** A good seal is crucial for safe preservation. If a jar does not seal properly, refrigerate it and consume the contents within a few days.
- **Use the Right Equipment:** While you can technically use any large pot for water bath canning, a dedicated canner with a rack will make your life easier.

And there you have it, folks, a primer on the handy, straightforward method of water bath canning. It's a skill that'll allow you to preserve a bounty of foods for your pantry, ensuring you'll have access to delicious, homemade goods all year round. Now let's turn our attention to pressure canning.

PRESSURE CANNING

Now let's a deep dive into a method of canning that's essential for safely preserving low-acid foods such as meats, poultry, vegetables, and chili: pressure canning.

It might seem a little intimidating at first, but once you've got the hang of it, you'll wonder how you ever lived without it. Let's get started!

The Basics of Pressure Canning

Unlike water bath canning, pressure canning allows you to reach higher temperatures (up to 240 degrees Fahrenheit). This is crucial for safely preserving low-acid foods, as these higher temperatures are needed to kill off harmful bacteria and other microorganisms.

Here's a step-by-step guide:

1. **Prepare Your Ingredients:** Clean, peel, chop, or otherwise prepare your food according to your chosen recipe.
2. **Prepare Your Jars and Lids:** Sterilize your jars, lids, and bands by washing in warm, soapy water.
3. **Fill Your Jars:** Pack your food into the jars, leaving enough headspace (usually about 1 inch) at the top.
4. **Seal Your Jars:** Wipe the rim of the jar to ensure a clean seal. Place a sterilized lid on the jar and screw on the band until it's finger-tight.
5. **Process Your Jars:** Place your jars in the pressure canner, seal the canner, and bring the water to a boil. Once steam begins to vent, allow it to continue for about 10 minutes, then apply the pressure regulator and begin processing.
6. **Cool and Check Your Jars:** Once processing time is up, let the canner cool and depressurize naturally. Then remove the jars using a jar lifter and let them cool for 12-24 hours. Check that the lids have sealed properly (they should not flex up and down when pressed). Store in a cool, dark place.

Best Foods for Pressure Canning

Pressure canning is ideal for low-acid foods, which include:

- Meats and poultry
- Seafood
- Vegetables like beans, peas, corn, carrots, and potatoes
- Soups and stews
- Chili

Pressure Canning Tips

To ensure success and safety in your pressure canning efforts, remember these tips:

- **Read the Manual:** If you're new to pressure canning or using a new pressure canner, always read the manual to understand how to use it safely.
- **Adjust for Altitude**: Like with water bath canning, the boiling point decreases as altitude increases, so adjust your processing time if you live at a high altitude.
- **Cool Naturally:** Never try to speed up the cooling or depressurizing process. This could lead to unsealed jars or, worse, a dangerous accident.
- **Check Seals:** If a jar doesn't seal properly, refrigerate it and consume the contents within a few days.

And there we have it! With the ability to safely preserve meats, veggies, and hearty stews, pressure canning adds depth to your food storage, ensuring you're well-equipped with a diverse range of nutritious foods.

Chapter Three: Freezing

Ah, freezing - nature's pause button. It's a method we all use, whether it's for preserving the last slice of birthday cake or prepping meals for the week. But did you know that freezing has been used as a preservation method since ancient times? Let's take a closer look.

The Ancient Origins of Freezing

If you think about it, freezing as a method of food preservation is as old as winter itself. Ancient civilizations living in cold climates, such as the Inuit in the Arctic and the Mongols on the Asian steppes, used freezing as their primary method of preserving food. They would freeze fish, meat, and even berries to ensure a steady food supply through the long winter months.

Sure, they didn't have frost-free freezers or vacuum sealers, but they had blistering cold, snow-packed storage pits, and ice houses to do the job. Today, we've taken this time-tested method and tweaked it to suit our modern lives.

Modern Freezing Techniques and Tips

In our modern world, freezing is as easy as tossing a bag of peas into the freezer. But to get the best results, there are a few tricks to the trade:

1. **Blanch before freezing**: For vegetables, blanching (briefly boiling) before freezing can help maintain color, texture, and nutritional value.
2. **Cool before freezing**: Let cooked food cool before you freeze it. Putting hot food directly in the freezer can increase the overall temperature, affecting other stored items.
3. **Portion wisely**: Freeze food in meal-sized portions for easy thawing and use.
4. **Vacuum sealing**: If you have a vacuum sealer, use it. It's not essential, but it can prevent freezer burn and help your food last longer.

Freezing Different Food Types

Just about any food can be frozen, but some fare better than others. Here's a quick guide:

- **Fruits and Vegetables:** Best when blanched first, but most can be frozen raw. Berries, in particular, freeze beautifully.
- **Meats and Fish**: Freeze at the peak of freshness. Thaw in the fridge to prevent bacterial growth.
- **Breads and Baked Goods**: Can be frozen, though texture may be slightly affected upon thawing.

- **Dairy Products:** Some, like butter and cheese, freeze well. Others, like milk and cream, may separate but are still safe to use.

Recipes for Freezer-ready Meals

Ready to fill your freezer with some delicious, ready-to-go meals? Here are a couple of my favorite freezer-friendly recipes.

Hearty Vegetable Soup: A versatile recipe where you can toss in any veggies you have on hand. Cook a big batch, let it cool, portion it out, and freeze. Perfect for those cold winter nights when you need a warm hug in a bowl.

Marinated Chicken: Mix up your favorite marinade, add your chicken pieces, and freeze. When you're ready to use, just thaw in the fridge overnight, and it's ready to grill, bake, or stir-fry.

Remember, friend, freezing may be easy, but doing it right can mean the difference between a delicious home-cooked meal and a sad, frostbitten lump of ice.

Keep the spirit of our ancestors in mind, respect the food, and freezing will serve you well. Stay cool, and join me next time as we dive into the salty world of curing and smoking.

Chapter Four: Curing

Ah, curing - the ancient method that gave us delectable treats like bacon, ham, and prosciutto. There's something profoundly satisfying about turning a fresh piece of meat into a shelf-stable, flavor-packed delicacy. Let's dig in, shall we?

The Ancient Art of Curing

Curing has been around for thousands of years. Before refrigeration and canning, it was one of the primary ways our ancestors preserved their meat. They discovered that by applying salt and other ingredients, they could prevent spoilage and create a product that not only lasted longer but tasted great too.

The art of curing has been refined over the centuries and varies from culture to culture. Think of Spanish jamón, Italian salami, American country ham, or Chinese lap yuk. Each has its own unique flavor profile, yet they all share the same basic principles of curing.

Ingredients Used in Curing

At its most basic, curing requires only one ingredient: salt. Salt dehydrates the meat, creating an environment where bacteria can't thrive. However, modern curing often incorporates a few other ingredients to enhance flavor and safety:

1. **Curing Salts:** These are special salts that contain nitrites or nitrates, which prevent the growth of harmful bacteria and give cured meats their characteristic pink color.
2. **Sugar:** Used to balance the harshness of the salt and to aid in the fermentation process in some types of cured meats.

3. **Spices and Flavorings:** These can vary widely depending on the recipe. Anything from black pepper to juniper berries to maple syrup can be used to flavor the meat.

The Curing Process: A Step-by-Step Guide

Ready to try your hand at curing? Here's a simplified guide to get you started:

1. **Choose Your Meat:** This could be anything from a pork belly for bacon to a whole ham. Just make sure it's fresh and of good quality.
2. **Prepare Your Cure:** Mix your curing ingredients according to your recipe. This often involves combining salt, curing salts, sugar, and any desired flavorings.
3. **Apply the Cure:** Coat your meat thoroughly with the cure.

4. **Rest and Wait:** Place the meat in a sealable bag or covered container in the fridge. Now comes the hard part: waiting. The curing process can take anywhere from a few days to several weeks.
5. **Rinse and Dry:** Once cured, rinse off the excess salt and pat dry. Some cured meats may be used right away, while others may need additional aging or cooking.

Tips and Recipes for Curing Meats and Fish

Curing is as much an art as it is a science, and it can take some practice to get it just right. Here are a few tips:

- **Safety First:** Always use curing salts with caution and according to the package instructions.
- **Patience is Key:** Curing can't be rushed. Trust the process and give your meat the time it needs.
- **Experiment with Flavors:** Once you've mastered the basics, feel free to play around with different spices and flavorings to make the recipe your own.

For your first curing adventure, why not try a simple dry-cured bacon? It's surprisingly easy to make and the results are so much more flavorful than store-bought bacon. Plus, who doesn't love bacon?

Now that you're armed with the knowledge of curing, I'll leave you to turn your kitchen into a curing chamber. Join me in the next chapter where we'll heat things up with smoking. Until then, keep things salty!

Chapter Five: Smoking

We've salted, frozen, and canned our way through the food preservation world, and now we've arrived at the deliciously aromatic realm of smoking. Buckle up, as we dive into the haze of this ancient food tradition.

The Tradition of Smoking Food

Smoking food is an age-old method, likely discovered accidentally when our ancestors found that foods hung near the fire took on a pleasing flavor and lasted longer. For thousands of years, communities from all over the globe have used smoke to preserve and flavor foods ranging from meat and fish to cheese and even beverages.

Just like curing, smoking techniques vary across different cultures. But no matter where you are in the world, the basic principle remains the same: exposing food to smoke to enhance its taste and prolong its shelf-life.

Building or Choosing a Smoker

Whether you're ready to build a professional smokehouse in your backyard or just want to get started with a simple setup, here's what you need to consider:

1. **Space**: How much room do you have? This will dictate the size of the smoker you can accommodate.
2. **Budget:** Smokers range from inexpensive DIY options to top-of-the-line commercial units. Determine what you're willing to spend.
3. **Type of Smoker:** From traditional wood-burning smokers to electric and gas models, each comes with its own pros and cons. Research to find out which one suits your needs and preferences.
4. **Temperature Control:** Regardless of the type of smoker, it's crucial to have reliable temperature control for successful smoking.

Smoking Techniques for Different Foods

Smoking techniques can vary based on the type of food, the desired flavor, and the specific tradition or style you're following. Here's a basic guideline:

- **Meats and Fish:** These are usually cured first, then smoked. The smoking process can take anywhere from a few hours to several days, depending on the size of the piece and the desired flavor intensity.
- **Cheese:** Cold smoking is used for cheese to infuse flavor without melting the product.

- **Vegetables and Nuts:** These can also be smoked to add a depth of flavor that's usually hard to achieve with these ingredients.

Recipes for Smoked Delicacies

Now that you've got the basics, let's dive into a couple of recipes to get you started:

Smoked Salmon: A classic smoked dish, smoked salmon requires a good brine before being slow-smoked to perfection.

Applewood Smoked Chicken: A whole chicken, marinated and smoked over applewood chips, creates a mouth-watering meal with a delicate smoky flavor.

Remember, smoking is an art, and like all arts, it requires practice. Don't be discouraged if your first few attempts don't yield the desired results. Keep experimenting, keep learning, and most importantly, have fun!

Next time, we'll be moving on to another form of food preservation that's equally exciting - salting. Until then, keep those smoke signals coming!

Chapter Six: Salting

We've journeyed through canning, freezing, curing, and smoking, and now it's time to venture into a method that's as old as civilization itself - salting. Let's dive into the world of preserving food with this humble yet powerful ingredient.

The History and Importance of Salting

From the ancient Egyptians to the Romans and medieval Europeans, people around the globe have been using salt to preserve food for millennia. Salt was so valuable in many cultures it was even used as currency. You can see how crucial it was not only for enhancing flavor but also for sustaining civilization by enabling long voyages and surviving harsh winters.

Salt works by drawing out moisture from food, creating an environment inhospitable to bacteria, yeast, and molds that cause food spoilage. It's a simple method, but highly effective.

How to Salt Different Foods

Salting can be as straightforward as packing food in salt (dry salting) or submerging it in a brine (wet salting). The method you choose will depend on the type of food you're preserving:

- **Meat and Fish:** Can be dry salted or brined. Often these are then dried, smoked, or cooked for added flavor and preservation.
- **Vegetables:** Typically preserved using a method called lacto-fermentation, where salt encourages the growth of beneficial bacteria that preserve and flavor the food.

Advantages and Limitations of Salting

Salting has many benefits: it's economical, requires no special equipment, enhances flavor, and has a long track record of safety. However, there are a few downsides:

- **Salty Flavor:** Some may find the flavor too strong. Often, salted foods are soaked or cooked to reduce the saltiness.
- **Nutrient Loss:** Some vitamins can be lost during salting.
- **Storage**: Salted foods often require specific storage conditions to prevent spoilage or becoming overly desiccated.

Salting Recipes to Try at Home

Ready to get started? Here are a couple of simple recipes:

1. **Corned Beef:** A delicious example of wet salting, corned beef is soaked in a spiced brine for several days before being slow-cooked to perfection.

2. **Sauerkraut:** A classic lacto-fermented dish, sauerkraut is nothing more than cabbage and salt, yet the resulting flavor is complex and tangy.

Remember, the key to successful salting is the quality of the ingredients and patience. It's a slow process, but the rewards are worth it.

Chapter Seven: Dehydrating

Our food preservation journey continues and this time, we're entering a terrain that's as old as the sun - dehydration. It's time to take a closer look at this timeless food preservation method.

Dehydration: The Oldest Method of Food Preservation

Long before we developed canning, freezing, or even salting, our ancestors used the sun and wind to dry their foods, preserving them for leaner times. Dehydration works by removing the water content from food, which inhibits the growth of bacteria, yeasts, and molds.

While the traditional sun-drying method is still used in many parts of the world, we now have modern dehydrators that can dry foods efficiently while maintaining their nutritional content.

Choosing a Dehydrator: Tips and Recommendations

When it comes to choosing a dehydrator, consider the following factors:

1. **Size and Capacity:** How much food do you plan on dehydrating at a time?
2. **Adjustable Temperature Control:** Different foods require different drying temperatures, so this feature is a must.
3. **Even Airflow:** Look for a model that promotes even airflow across all trays for consistent drying.

4. **Ease of Cleaning:** Dehydrating can be a messy business, so opt for a model that's easy to clean.

The Dehydration Process: A Step-by-Step Guide

While dehydrating is a relatively straightforward process, there are a few key steps to ensure success:

- **Preparation:** Wash, peel (if necessary), and cut your food into uniform slices to ensure even drying.
- **Pre-treatment:** Some foods, like apples and pears, may need to be pre-treated to prevent browning. Blanching can be used for some vegetables to halt enzyme activity and help retain color and nutrients.
- **Drying:** Arrange the food on the dehydrator trays, ensuring pieces don't overlap. Set the temperature and timer according to the manufacturer's recommendations or your recipe.
- **Conditioning and Storing:** Once dried, let the food cool, then store it in airtight containers in a cool, dark location.

Dehydrating Different Foods: Recipes and Tips

Just about any food can be dehydrated, but here are a few favorites to get you started:

Fruit Leathers: Puree your favorite fruits, spread the puree on a dehydrator sheet, and dry to make your own healthy, portable snacks.

Jerky: Slice lean meat, marinate it in your favorite flavors, and dehydrate it to make homemade jerky.

Herbs: Dehydrate fresh herbs like rosemary, thyme, or mint for a year-round supply of flavor for your dishes.

Remember, the secret to successful dehydration is patience. Don't try to speed up the process by increasing the temperature, as this can result in unevenly dried food. Take your time, and let the warm, gentle breeze of your dehydrator work its magic.

Chapter Eight: Fermenting

We've ventured through an array of preservation techniques so far, and now it's time to bubble into the effervescent world of fermenting. Let's unlock the power of this microscopic wonderland!

The Ancient Practice of Fermentation

Long before we understood the science behind it, our ancestors discovered that leaving certain foods in a controlled environment resulted in a unique, often tangy, flavor. This, my friends, was the discovery of fermentation.

From the briny tang of sauerkraut to the effervescent zip of kombucha, fermentation brings not just extended shelf life, but also a wealth of flavors to foods and drinks. At its core, fermentation is the process where microorganisms, like yeast and bacteria, convert sugars into other substances such as alcohol, gases, or acids, thereby preserving the food.

Health Benefits of Fermented Foods

Fermented foods aren't just delicious—they're also packed with health benefits. They contain probiotics, beneficial bacteria that can improve digestion, boost immunity, and even enhance mood.

In addition, the fermentation process can increase the bioavailability of nutrients in food, making them easier for our bodies to absorb. That's a big win-win in my book!

Step-by-Step Fermenting Process

Though the specifics of fermenting can vary based on the type of food you're working with, here's a basic guide:

- **Preparation**: Chop or shred your chosen food. Some recipes might require the addition of a brine or a starter culture.
- **Pack:** Pack your food tightly into a clean jar to minimize air exposure. The food should be completely submerged in the liquid.
- **Wait**: Store the jar at room temperature out of direct sunlight and give nature time to do its thing. Depending on the recipe, this could take anywhere from a few days to several weeks.
- **Check and Store:** Once the fermentation is to your liking, store the jar in the refrigerator to slow down the fermentation process.

Fermenting Recipes from Around the World

Fermentation is a global affair, with unique recipes hailing from all corners of the world. Here are a few to get you started:

- **Sauerkraut:** This German staple is simply fermented cabbage and salt. Simple to make, packed with flavor and healthy to boot.
- **Kimchi:** This spicy Korean delicacy usually features cabbage, radishes, and a mix of flavorful seasonings.
- **Sourdough Bread**: The tangy, chewy delight that is sourdough bread begins with a simple fermented mixture of flour and water known as a 'starter'.

Remember, fermenting is a living process and each batch may be a little different. That's part of the charm!

It's an exciting, delicious, and health-boosting way to preserve food.

Chapter Nine: Pickling

We've traveled through a myriad of preservation methods, and we've finally arrived at the zingy, tangy domain of pickling. Whether you're a dill devotee or a sweet gherkin fan, we're going to delve into all things pickled!

The Art and Science of Pickling

Pickling, much like fermenting, involves creating an environment where good bacteria thrive and the bad bacteria that spoil food can't survive. The main difference is the introduction of an acidic solution, often vinegar, which kickstarts the preservation and flavoring process.

Pickling is practiced around the globe, from the kosher dills of New York delis to the pickled ginger served with sushi in Japan. Despite the differences, the core of pickling remains the same: it's the art of preserving food in a brine or an acidic solution, yielding a tangy delight that can jazz up any meal.

Necessary Equipment and Ingredients for Pickling

Let's start with the basics. Here's what you'll need:

- **Jars:** Glass jars with tight-fitting lids are ideal for pickling.

- **Vinegar:** This is the foundation of your pickling liquid. White vinegar is commonly used, but apple cider, red wine, and other vinegars can add unique flavors.
- **Salt:** Pickling or kosher salt is best as they're free of additives.
- **Sugar:** Depending on the recipe, sugar can be used to balance the acidity.
- **Spices:** This is where you can get creative. Mustard seeds, peppercorns, dill, garlic, and bay leaves are common, but feel free to experiment.
- **The Star of the Show:** The food you want to pickle! Cucumbers, onions, and carrots are traditional, but don't be afraid to try other fruits and veggies.

The Pickling Process: A Detailed Guide

Here's a basic pickling process:

1. **Prepare Your Produce:** Clean and cut your produce. For crunchier pickles, leave the skins on.
2. **Prepare the Brine:** Combine vinegar, water, and any salt or sugar in a saucepan and bring to a boil.
3. **Pack the Jars:** Place your spices and produce in the jars, then pour over the hot brine, leaving a bit of space at the top.
4. **Seal and Wait:** Once the jars are sealed, let them cool to room temperature. Then, refrigerate them. Most pickles will be ready to eat after a few days, but they'll continue to develop flavor over time.

Traditional and Innovative Pickling Recipes

Now you're ready to dive into pickling! Here are a couple of recipes to kick-start your pickling journey:

- **Classic Dill Pickles:** These are a staple in the pickling world. All you need are cucumbers, dill, garlic, water, vinegar, and pickling salt.
- **Pickled Red Onions:** A simple and delicious condiment that can elevate any dish. Plus, they turn a beautiful pink color that's sure to impress.

- **Sweet Pickled Watermelon Rinds:** Yes, you read that right! This Southern classic is a perfect example of food preservation at its most creative and waste-free.

Remember, patience is key in pickling. The longer you wait, the more the flavors will develop.

Soon enough, you'll have a pantry full of brightly colored, tangy delights ready to accompany your meals.

Chapter Ten: Complete Meals in a Jar

Let's now explore a fantastic, ready-to-go solution for long-term food storage - complete meals in a jar. Imagine having a variety of meals, waiting on the shelf, just a heating source away from being served.

Not only are these great for crisis situations, but they also come in handy for those days when you don't feel like cooking. So, without further ado, let's get to the nitty-gritty of crafting meals in a jar.

The Basics of Meal Preparation in a Jar

The process of creating a meal in a jar is relatively simple: combine all the dried ingredients of your meal into a jar, then seal and store. When ready to eat, add water, cook, and voila! You have a hot, ready-to-eat meal. Here are the general steps:

- **Choose Your Recipe:** The first step is selecting a recipe. Soups, stews, and casseroles often work well.
- **Prepare Your Ingredients:** This is where your preservation skills truly shine. Dehydrate or dry-can the ingredients as needed.
- **Layer Your Ingredients:** Carefully layer your ingredients into the jar. This not only looks appealing, but it also makes it easier to ensure you have the right amounts of each ingredient.

- **Seal Your Jar:** Once all ingredients are in the jar, you need to seal it. For dry ingredients, you can use an oxygen absorber before sealing the jar to extend shelf life.
- **Store Your Meal:** Finally, store your jar in a cool, dark, dry place.

Tips and Tricks for Successful Meal Jars

Here are some insights to ensure your jar meals are a resounding success:

- **Ingredient Selection:** Choose ingredients that have similar rehydration times. This ensures that all components of your meal will be ready to eat at the same time.
- **Include a Recipe:** Attach a recipe to each jar that includes any necessary additional ingredients and cooking instructions.
- **Think About Nutrition:** Aim to include a good mix of proteins, carbohydrates, and vegetables in each jar to ensure a well-rounded meal.
- **Shelf Life:** While these meals can last a long time on the shelf, it's important to note that they won't last indefinitely. Check the expiration dates of your individual ingredients to get a rough idea of the meal's shelf life.

Sample Meals in a Jar Recipes

To get you started, here are a few simple, hearty meals that work great in a jar:

- **Chicken Soup:** Layer dehydrated chicken, dried veggies (carrots, peas, corn, onions), rice, and your favorite herbs and spices.
- **Chili:** Layer dried beans, dehydrated ground beef, dried onions, dehydrated bell peppers, and a spice mix of chili powder, cumin, garlic powder, and salt.
- **Pasta Primavera:** Layer dehydrated veggies (broccoli, bell peppers, onions, tomatoes), pasta, dried cheese, and Italian seasoning.

Meals in a jar are a perfect blend of convenience and nutrition, stored neatly in a compact, shelf-stable format.

They truly exemplify the spirit of preparation and self-reliance, ensuring you'll have a home-cooked meal ready, even in the toughest of times.

Chapter Eleven: Food Safety and Storage

As we round out this enlightening journey through the annals of food preservation, we need to touch on one crucial aspect: food safety and storage.

When handled correctly, preserved foods can be a reliable, nutritious part of your stockpile. But to ensure these jars, bags, and containers are truly blessings and not hidden time-bombs of spoilage, we need to take certain precautions.

Ensuring Safety in Food Preservation

There's an old saying among us food preservation enthusiasts: "When in doubt, throw it out." If something smells funky or looks off, don't take chances. Here are a few key points to keep in mind:

- **Cleanliness:** Make sure your work area, tools, and containers are all clean. And don't forget about your hands!
- **Follow Recipes:** Stick to tested recipes, especially when canning. Altering the ingredients can change acidity levels and lead to unsafe food.
- **Check Seals:** Before consuming home-canned goods, check that the seal is still intact. A broken or bulging lid can indicate spoilage.

- **Proper Handling:** Some foods, like meat or dairy, require specific handling to prevent bacterial growth. Always follow guidelines for these foods.

Best Practices for Long-Term Storage

After going to all the effort of preserving your food, you want it to stay good for as long as possible. Here's how:

- **Cool, Dark, Dry:** Store preserved foods in a cool, dark, dry place. Excessive heat and light can degrade food quality and even lead to spoilage.
- **Categorize and Label:** Label each jar or package with the contents and the date it was preserved. Keeping similar items together can also make it easier to find what you need.
- **Use Proper Containers:** Some foods store best in certain types of containers. For example, glass jars are great for most canned goods, while vacuum-sealed bags or airtight containers are best for dehydrated foods.

Managing and Rotating Your Stockpile

A key part of food storage is rotation. The rule here is "first in, first out." Use your oldest items first and move newer items to the back. Regularly check your stockpile for any signs of spoilage or pests and to keep an inventory of what you have.

Remember, stockpiling isn't a "set it and forget it" task. It's an ongoing process of adding, using, and monitoring your supplies. Treat it like your very own grocery store, where freshness and variety are king.

Chapter Twelve: Food Preservation in a Grid-Down Situation

Now that we've explored various methods of food preservation, let's take a step further and envision a scenario where modern amenities are unavailable. A grid-down situation could be anything from a power outage to a more severe, long-term event. But, fear not! Our ancestors have left us with a bounty of wisdom. Let's dive into how they employed these techniques without modern conveniences.

Harnessing Nature: Curing and Smoking

In the absence of refrigeration, curing and smoking were key techniques to preserve meat and fish. Salt, a natural preservative, was used extensively in curing. The removal of moisture through salting created an environment unsuitable for the growth of spoilage bacteria. And if salt was scarce, they would use the power of smoke.

The smoking process was achieved by hanging the food above a smoky fire. The smoke provided not only flavor but also added preservation properties. This process required a lot of care and attention, but it allowed them to store foods for extended periods.

The Art of Fermenting and Pickling

Fermenting was a widespread method our ancestors used to preserve a variety of foods. They often stored fermented food in earthenware crocks, which were placed in cool, dark cellars to maintain a consistent temperature. Kimchi in Korea, sauerkraut in Europe, and many more fermented foods came into being this way.

Pickling, like fermenting, utilized nature's own preservatives — vinegar or brine — to keep food edible for longer periods. Using barrels, crocks, or other containers, vegetables were submerged in the pickling solution and stored away for future use.

Natural Cold Storage: Freezing

While our ancestors didn't have modern freezers, they were no strangers to the concept of freezing. In cold climates, they would take advantage of the winter months to freeze and store food. Ice houses and cellars were often used to store frozen goods and to prolong the freezing period as far into the warmer months as possible.

Sun-Powered Dehydration

Before electric dehydrators, the sun and air were the best resources for drying food. Our ancestors would lay out thinly sliced food on screens or clean cloths and let the warmth of the sun slowly dry them out. This process required dry, warm weather and usually took several days.

Putting Up Food: Canning

While canning seems inherently modern, early forms of this preservation method date back to the 18th century. Instead of pressure canners, they used large boiling water baths. Jars were capped with wax seals or glass lids held in place with metal clamps, creating the necessary vacuum seal for preservation.

Safe Storage Practices

Even without modern conveniences, our ancestors understood the importance of proper storage. They kept their preserved goods in cellars, caves, or other cool, dry places, protected from direct sunlight and pests.

Though we enjoy the convenience of modern appliances, it's empowering to know that we can turn back the clock and use these age-old methods to preserve food when necessary.

Our ancestors have gifted us the knowledge; it's up to us to keep these traditions alive, ensuring our survival and self-sufficiency in any circumstance. As we part ways, remember this: with these skills under your belt, you're not just prepared, you're unstoppable!

Chapter Thirteen: DIY Survival Food Buckets

In this chapter, we're venturing into a vital part of any long-term survival plan: creating your own survival food buckets. These buckets are jam-packed with preserved food, capable of feeding you and your loved ones for an extended period, be it during a crisis or just an ordinary day. Let's dive into how to prepare and pack these buckets for years of safe storage.

The Basics of Survival Food Buckets

Survival food buckets are large, typically 5-gallon, food-grade buckets filled with a variety of preserved foods. The goal is to provide a long-lasting supply of balanced, nutritious meals that require minimal preparation – usually just water.

Assembling Your Survival Food Buckets

Here's a simple guide to assembling your own survival food buckets:

1. **Choose Your Bucket:** You want to use a food-grade plastic bucket with a sealable lid. A 5-gallon bucket is standard because it's big enough to hold a substantial amount of food but small enough to be portable.
2. **Select Your Food:** Focus on long-lasting, nutritious, and easy-to-prepare items. These can include:
    a. Dried goods: pasta, rice, lentils, beans
    b. Dehydrated or freeze-dried fruits and vegetables
    c. Dehydrated meats

d. Powdered dairy products: milk, cheese
  e. Sealed cans or pouches of meats, fruits, and vegetables
  f. Packets of spices, bouillon cubes, salt, and sugar
3. **Pack Your Food:** If not already packaged for long-term storage, place your food in airtight Mylar bags with oxygen absorbers to extend shelf life. Seal these bags with a heat sealer.
4. **Organize Your Bucket:** Pack the heaviest items at the bottom of the bucket and fill the rest of the space with lighter items. Try to maximize space and limit the movement of items within the bucket.
5. **Seal and Store:** Once packed, seal the bucket tightly. Store it in a cool, dry place away from sunlight.

Survival Food Bucket Tips

Here are a few tips to make your survival food bucket more effective:

- **Variety is Key**: Pack a range of foods to avoid "menu fatigue" – that is, getting bored with your food choices. Remember, you might be relying on these buckets for an extended period.
- **Don't Forget Water:** You'll need plenty of water to rehydrate and cook many of these foods, so be sure to include water storage and purification methods in your overall survival plan.
- **Rotate Your Stock:** Keep track of the shelf life of your food items and rotate your stock accordingly. This will ensure that your food is always safe to eat when you need it.
- **Include a Can Opener:** If you're including canned goods, toss in a manual can opener. It's easy to forget, but essential in a grid-down situation.

Creating your own survival food buckets is a practical and economical way to prepare for uncertain times. Plus, it gives you the chance to tailor the contents to your family's needs and preferences.

Chapter Fourteen: Safeguarding Your Food Supply

In this chapter, we'll delve into a critical yet often overlooked topic – safeguarding your precious preserved food supplies. In a crisis situation, your stockpile becomes an invaluable resource. Protecting it from potential threats, such as theft or confiscation, becomes paramount. Let's delve into effective storage and camouflage techniques to ensure your hard work doesn't fall into the wrong hands.

Secure Storage Solutions

Here's the first line of defense: storing your food in a secure, inconspicuous location. But remember, your stash should be easily accessible to you and your loved ones.

- **Basements and Cellars:** These spaces offer ideal conditions for many preserved foods – they're dark, cool, and usually overlooked.
- **False Panels and Hidden Rooms**: You can create secret storage areas behind false panels in walls or underneath floors. If you're handy, you might even consider constructing a hidden room.
- **Furniture with Hidden Compartments**: A practical yet sneaky solution. Think a bookshelf with a secret cavity or a bed with a hidden storage unit underneath.

Dispersed Storage

Rather than storing all your food in one place, consider spreading it out. This way, if one stash is discovered, all is not lost.

- **Multiple Locations:** Use various spots around your home, yard, or property. Think creatively, like an old, unused well, a hollow tree, or a disguised garden shed.
- **Underground Caches:** These are containers that are weatherproof and can be buried. You can use PVC pipes capped at both ends, metal ammunition boxes, or commercially available caching tubes.

Camouflage Techniques

You'll also want to make your food stores blend seamlessly into their surroundings.

- **Natural Camouflage**: If you're storing food outside, consider using the natural landscape for camouflage. Bury caches near landmarks that are easy for you to identify but would look nondescript to others.
- **Everyday Items**: Inside your home, you can hide food inside other containers. A large, labeled dog food bag, for instance, could contain vacuum-sealed packages of rice or beans.

Operational Security (OPSEC)

This term, commonly used in military circles, refers to the idea of safeguarding information that could be used against you. Simply put, don't let others know about your food stores. The fewer people who know about your supplies, the less likely they are to be stolen or confiscated.

Remember, while these methods can provide additional security, they're not foolproof. The key is to be creative, adaptable, and always aware of your surroundings.

By taking these measures, you can sleep a bit easier, knowing that your preserved foods are as safe and secure as possible.

Chapter Fifteen: Conclusion

Well, we've made quite the journey, haven't we? From the canning pot to the dehydrator, from the pickling jar to the salt cure, we've traversed the fascinating landscape of food preservation, just like our ancestors did. In this concluding chapter, we'll reflect on the role of these techniques in the context of modern self-reliance, preparedness, and sustainability.

Food Preservation: A Pillar of Self-Reliance

In our technology-dependent society, it's easy to forget that not so long ago, knowing how to preserve food was a survival necessity. But the preppers and survivalists among us know that relying solely on modern conveniences is a vulnerable position to be in.

Food preservation skills can be a lifeline in times of crisis, whether it's a natural disaster, a power grid failure, or even a global pandemic. These methods not only allow you to have food on hand when grocery store shelves are bare but also provide you with nutritious, home-cooked meals instead of a diet solely dependent on processed, store-bought goods.

The Culture of Preparedness and Sustainability

Embracing food preservation encourages a mindset of preparedness. It prompts us to think ahead, to consider what-if scenarios and to plan accordingly. This kind of foresight is invaluable, not just in emergency situations, but in everyday life.

Moreover, food preservation contributes to a more sustainable lifestyle. When you preserve what you grow in your garden or buy from local farmers in season, you're reducing your carbon footprint. You're also combating food waste - one of the most significant issues our world faces today.

Looking Ahead

As we've seen in this book, food preservation isn't just about survival; it's about enhancing the quality of life. Imagine opening a jar of summer-ripe peaches in the dead of winter or enjoying home-cured ham on a family camping trip. Imagine the peace of mind knowing you have a well-stocked pantry, ready for whatever may come.

If there's one key message to take from this book, it's this: Food preservation skills are not only relevant but are vital, now more than ever. They empower us, helping us become more self-reliant and less dependent on an often unpredictable food supply chain.

So, my friends, let's keep this culture of preparedness alive. Let's pass these skills down to future generations. Let's continue to learn, innovate, and share within our community. For in the world of food preservation, there's always something new to discover, a recipe to perfect, a technique to master.

Thank you for joining me on this incredible journey. Now, go forth, stock your pantry, and remember: in the world of self-reliance, your greatest asset is your knowledge.

Stay prepared and keep preserving!

BONUS: 50 Meal in a Jar Recipes!

Name	Meal Type	Ingredients	Instructions
"Morning Sunshine" Breakfast Jar	Breakfast	- 1/3 cup instant oats - 1 tbsp chia seeds - 1/4 cup dried berries - 1/2 cup powdered milk	Layer ingredients in jar. To prepare, add warm water, stir, and let sit for a few minutes until oats and chia seeds have softened.
"Sunshine Cereal" Breakfast Jar	Breakfast	- 1/2 cup instant oats - 1/4 cup dried fruit - 2 tbsp honey granules	Add hot water to the jar, stir, and let sit for a few minutes until everything is well mixed and soft.
"Berry Good" Oatmeal Jar	Breakfast	- 1/2 cup instant oats - 1/4 cup dried berries - 2 tbsp honey granules	Add hot water to the jar, stir, and let sit for a few minutes until the oats are soft.
"Choco-Berry" Breakfast Jar	Breakfast	- 1/2 cup instant oats - 1/4 cup dried berries - 2 tbsp cocoa powder	Add hot water to the jar, stir, and let sit for a few minutes until the oats are soft.
"Sweet Morning" Granola Jar	Breakfast	- 1/2 cup granola - 1/4 cup dried fruit - 2 tbsp honey granules	Add cold milk or yogurt to the jar and let sit for a few minutes until the granola is slightly softened.
"Tropical Paradise" Breakfast Jar	Breakfast	- 1/2 cup instant oats - 1/4 cup dried tropical fruits (like pineapple, mango) - 2 tbsp coconut flakes	Add hot water to the jar, stir, and let sit for a few minutes until the oats are soft.
"Hearty Morning" Breakfast Jar	Breakfast	- 1/2 cup instant oats - 1/4 cup dried nuts - 2 tbsp honey granules	Add hot water to the jar, stir, and let sit for a few minutes until the oats are soft.
"Fruity Morning" Breakfast Jar	Breakfast	- 1/2 cup instant oats - 1/4 cup dried mixed fruits - 2 tbsp honey granules	Add hot water to the jar, stir, and let sit for a few minutes until the oats are soft.
"Fruit Parfait" Jar (Dairy-free)	Breakfast/Dessert	- 1/2 cup granola - 1/4 cup mixed dried fruit - 1/4 cup dairy-free yogurt powder	Add cold water to the jar, stir, and let sit for a few minutes until the yogurt is rehydrated. Top with granola and dried fruit.
Brownie Mix Jar	Dessert	- 1 cup sugar - 1/2 cup cocoa powder -	Layer ingredients in jar. To prepare, mix with melted butter and eggs,

Name	Meal Type	Ingredients	Instructions
		1/2 cup flour - 1/2 cup chopped nuts	pour into a baking dish, and bake until set.
"Sweet Dreams" Dessert Jar	Dessert	- 1/2 cup instant vanilla pudding powder - 1/4 cup dried berries - 1/4 cup granola	Add cold milk to the jar, stir, and let sit for a few minutes until the pudding sets. Top with the granola.
"Easy Peasy" Lemon Squeezy Pie Jar	Dessert	- 1/2 cup instant lemon pudding powder - 1/4 cup graham cracker crumbs - 1/4 cup dried berries	Add cold milk to the jar, stir, and let sit for a few minutes until the pudding sets. Top with the crumbs and berries.
"Apple Pie" Dessert Jar	Dessert	- 1/2 cup dehydrated apples - 1/4 cup granola - 2 tbsp brown sugar	Add hot water to the jar and let it sit until the apples are rehydrated. Eat hot or cold.
"Berry Delight" Dessert Jar	Dessert	- 1/2 cup instant vanilla pudding powder - 1/4 cup dried mixed berries - 2 tbsp granola	Add cold milk to the jar, stir, and let sit for a few minutes until the pudding sets. Top with the granola.
"Chocolate Cherry" Dessert Jar	Dessert	- 1/2 cup instant chocolate pudding powder - 1/4 cup dried cherries - 2 tbsp chocolate granules	Add cold milk to the jar, stir, and let sit for a few minutes until the pudding sets.
"Caramel Apple" Dessert Jar	Dessert	- 1/2 cup dehydrated apples - 1/4 cup caramel bits - 1/4 cup granola	Add hot water to the jar and let it sit until the apples are rehydrated. Top with granola.
"Mixed Berry Compote" Jar (Dairy-free, Vegetarian)	Dessert	- 1/2 cup mixed dried berries - 1/4 cup sugar - 2 tbsp cornstarch	Add hot water to the jar, stir, and let sit for a few minutes until the berries are rehydrated. Heat on the stove until the mixture thickens.
Chili Mix Jar	Dinner	- 1/2 cup dried kidney beans - 1/4 cup dried ground beef - 2 tbsp chili powder	Layer ingredients in jar. To prepare, add to pot with water and simmer until beans are fully cooked and the chili is well heated.
"Burger and Fries" Soup Jar	Dinner	- 1/2 cup dehydrated ground beef - 1/4 cup dehydrated potatoes - 1/4 cup	Add hot water to the jar and let it sit until the ingredients are

Name	Meal Type	Ingredients	Instructions
		dehydrated vegetables	rehydrated. Heat on the stove until warm.
"Spicy Fiesta" Rice Jar	Dinner	- 1 cup instant rice - 1/4 cup dehydrated vegetables - 2 tbsp taco seasoning	Add hot water to the jar, stir, and let it sit until the rice and vegetables are rehydrated. Heat on the stove if desired.
"Italian Pasta" Jar	Dinner	- 1 cup pasta - 1/4 cup dehydrated vegetables - 1 tbsp Italian seasoning	Boil the contents of the jar until the pasta is cooked. Add a can of diced tomatoes and heat until everything is warmed through.
"Hearty Beef" Stew Jar	Dinner	- 1/2 cup dehydrated beef - 1/4 cup dehydrated vegetables - 1 tsp beef bouillon	Add hot water to the jar and let it sit until the ingredients are rehydrated. Heat on the stove until warm.
"Exotic Rice" Jar	Dinner	- 1 cup instant rice - 1/4 cup dehydrated vegetables - 2 tbsp curry powder	Add hot water to the jar, stir, and let it sit until the rice and vegetables are rehydrated. Heat on the stove if desired.
"Tex-Mex" Dinner Jar	Dinner	- 1/2 cup dehydrated ground beef - 1/4 cup dehydrated bell peppers - 2 tbsp taco seasoning	Add hot water to the jar and let it sit until the beef and bell peppers are rehydrated. Heat on the stove if desired.
"Asian Stir-Fry" Dinner Jar	Dinner	- 1 cup instant rice - 1/4 cup dehydrated mixed vegetables - 2 tbsp soy sauce granules	Add hot water to the jar, stir, and let it sit until the rice and vegetables are rehydrated. Heat on the stove if desired.
"Spicy Bean" Chili Jar	Dinner	- 1/2 cup dehydrated ground beef - 1/4 cup dehydrated beans - 2 tbsp chili seasoning	Add hot water to the jar and let it sit until the ingredients are rehydrated. Heat on the stove until warm.
"Mexican Fiesta" Rice Jar	Dinner	- 1 cup instant rice - 1/4 cup dehydrated mixed vegetables - 2 tbsp taco seasoning	Add hot water to the jar, stir, and let it sit until the rice and vegetables are rehydrated. Heat on the stove if desired.
"Vegan Curry" Jar (Dairy-free, Vegetarian)	Dinner	- 1 cup instant rice - 1/4 cup dehydrated mixed vegetables - 2 tbsp curry powder	Add hot water to the jar, stir, and let it sit until the rice and vegetables are rehydrated. Heat on the stove if desired.

Name	Meal Type	Ingredients	Instructions
"Rice & Beans" Jar (Dairy-free, Vegetarian)	Dinner	- 1/2 cup instant rice - 1/4 cup dehydrated beans - 2 tbsp taco seasoning	Add hot water to the jar and let it sit until the ingredients are rehydrated. Heat on the stove until warm.
"Veggie Fried Rice" Jar (Dairy-free, Vegetarian)	Dinner	- 1 cup instant rice - 1/4 cup dehydrated mixed vegetables - 2 tbsp soy sauce granules	Add hot water to the jar, stir, and let sit until the rice and vegetables are rehydrated. Heat on the stove
"Chicken Gravy with Rice" Jar	Dinner	- 1/2 cup instant rice - 1/4 cup dried chicken - 2 tbsp gravy granules	Add hot water to the jar, stir, and let sit for a few minutes until the rice and chicken are soft.
"Pot Roast and Gravy" Jar	Dinner	- 1/2 cup dehydrated beef - 1/4 cup dehydrated carrots and onions - 2 tbsp gravy granules	Add hot water to the jar and let it sit until the beef and vegetables are rehydrated. Heat on the stove if desired.
"Creamy Mushroom Rice" Jar	Dinner	- 1 cup instant rice - 1/4 cup dehydrated mushrooms - 2 tbsp cream of mushroom soup mix	Add hot water to the jar, stir, and let sit until the rice and mushrooms are rehydrated. Heat on the stove if desired.
"Beef Stroganoff" Jar	Dinner	- 1/2 cup dehydrated beef - 1/4 cup dehydrated mushrooms - 2 tbsp stroganoff sauce mix	Add hot water to the jar and let it sit until the ingredients are rehydrated. Heat on the stove until warm.
"Chicken and Rice Casserole" Jar	Dinner	- 1/2 cup instant rice - 1/4 cup dehydrated chicken - 1/4 cup dehydrated mixed vegetables	Add hot water to the jar, stir, and let sit until the rice, chicken, and vegetables are rehydrated. Heat on the stove if desired.
Couscous Salad Jar	Lunch	- 1/2 cup couscous - 1/4 cup dehydrated vegetables - 1 tbsp dried fruit	Add hot water to the jar, stir, and let sit for a few minutes until the couscous is fluffy.
"Greek Salad" Lunch Jar	Lunch	- 1/2 cup dehydrated cucumbers - 1/4 cup dehydrated tomatoes - 2 tbsp dried olives	Add cold water to the jar, stir, and let sit for a few minutes until the vegetables are rehydrated. Add some feta cheese if available.
Chicken Soup Jar	Lunch/Dinner	- 1/2 cup dehydrated vegetables - 1/4 cup dried chicken - 1 tsp	Layer ingredients in jar. To prepare, add boiling water, stir, and let sit for

Name	Meal Type	Ingredients	Instructions
		chicken bouillon powder	a few minutes until ingredients are rehydrated.
"Italian Night" Pasta Jar	Lunch/Dinner	- 1 cup pasta - 1/4 cup dehydrated vegetables - 1 tbsp Italian seasoning	Boil the contents of the jar until the pasta is cooked. Add a can of diced tomatoes and heat until everything is warmed through.
Veggie Soup Jar	Lunch/Dinner	- 1/2 cup dehydrated mixed vegetables - 1/4 cup dehydrated lentils - 1 tsp vegetable bouillon	Add hot water to the jar and let it sit until the vegetables and lentils are rehydrated. Heat on the stove if desired.
Quinoa Salad Jar	Lunch/Dinner	- 1/2 cup quinoa - 1/4 cup dehydrated vegetables - 1 tbsp dehydrated fruit (like cranberries)	Cook the quinoa and dehydrated vegetables in water until the quinoa is fluffy. Stir in the fruit. Eat hot or cold.
"Taco Tuesday" Soup Jar	Lunch/Dinner	- 1/2 cup dehydrated ground beef - 1/4 cup dehydrated black beans - 2 tbsp taco seasoning	Add hot water to the jar and let it sit until the ingredients are rehydrated. Heat on the stove until warm.
"Chicken Delight" Soup Jar	Lunch/Dinner	- 1/2 cup dehydrated chicken - 1/4 cup dehydrated mixed vegetables - 1 tsp chicken bouillon	Add hot water to the jar and let it sit until the chicken and vegetables are rehydrated. Heat on the stove if desired.
"Creamy Corn" Soup Jar	Lunch/Dinner	- 1/2 cup dehydrated corn - 1/4 cup instant mashed potatoes - 1 tsp vegetable bouillon	Add hot water to the jar and let it sit until the corn and potatoes are rehydrated. Heat on the stove until warm.
"Quinoa Veggie" Jar (Vegetarian)	Lunch/Dinner	- 1/2 cup quinoa - 1/4 cup dried mixed vegetables - 2 tbsp vegetable bouillon	Add hot water to the jar, stir, and let sit for a few minutes until the quinoa and vegetables are soft.
"Black Bean Soup" Jar (Vegetarian)	Lunch/Dinner	- 1/2 cup dehydrated black beans - 1/4 cup dehydrated mixed vegetables - 1 tsp vegetable bouillon	Add hot water to the jar and let it sit until the beans and vegetables are rehydrated. Heat on the stove if desired.
"Moroccan Lentil" Soup Jar (Vegetarian)	Lunch/Dinner	- 1/2 cup dehydrated lentils - 1/4 cup dehydrated carrots -	Add hot water to the jar and let it sit until the lentils and carrots are

Name	Meal Type	Ingredients	Instructions
		1 tsp vegetable bouillon	rehydrated. Heat on the stove until warm.
"Dairy-Free Creamy Broccoli Soup" Jar (Dairy-free)	Lunch/Dinner	- 1/2 cup dehydrated broccoli - 1/4 cup instant mashed potatoes - 1 tsp vegetable bouillon	Add hot water to the jar and let it sit until the broccoli and potatoes are rehydrated. Heat on the stove until warm.
"Vegetable Stew" Jar	Lunch/Dinner	- 1/2 cup mixed dehydrated vegetables - 1/4 cup dehydrated lentils - 2 tbsp vegetable bouillon	Add hot water to the jar, stir, and let sit for a few minutes until the vegetables and lentils are rehydrated.
"Chicken Noodle Soup" Jar	Lunch/Dinner	- 1/2 cup dehydrated chicken - 1/4 cup dehydrated mixed vegetables - 1/4 cup quick-cooking pasta	Add hot water to the jar and let it sit until the chicken and vegetables are rehydrated. Heat on the stove until warm.